Recorder from the Beginning

John Pitts

D0537469

To Caithin,

Happy Birthday &

Happy playing

lots of love

Auntie Jacqui :)

This recorder course in 2 stages has been designed for children aged 7 upwards. Since publication it has become one of the most popular schemes used in many parts of the world. **Recorder from the Beginning** assumes no previous knowledge of either music of the recorder, and full explanations are provided at every stage so that specialist teaching is not essential. Teacher's Books are available for each stage, and these contain simple piano accompaniments, guitar chord symbols and suggestions for each tune.

The new coloured edition of the books has allowed more emphasis on activities directly related to aspects of Music in the National Curriculum. For example opportunities are provided for recorder players to be accompanied by instrumental ostinati and other percussion accompaniments and for recorders to perform with singers in two-part items, rounds, songs with descants and other activities.

John Pitts 1993

Acknowledgements

The publishers would like to thank the following for permission to include their copyright material: The Society of Authors, as literary representatives of the estate of the late Rose Fyleman, the poem *Tadpoles*; Jan Holdstock, the words to *Traffic Jam*; Workers' Music Association, the melody of *The Fireman's not for me* from *the Shuttle and Cage* (Ewan MacColl); Jan Holdstock, the words and music of *Down in Bethlehem*. The music on the following pages has been specially composed and arranged for this book by the author: 4, 5, 6, 7, 8, 9, 10, 11, 12, 13, 16, 17, 18, 20, 21, 23, 26, 27, 32, 33(bottom), 34, 35, 36, 37(top), 38, 39, 40, 46, 55, 57(bottom), 61(bottom), 65, 67(bottom), 69(top), 72, 73, 78(bottom), 83, 85.

 OMNIBUS PRESS

Holding your recorder

Hold your recorder in front of you.
Put your left hand near the top.
Put your right hand near the bottom.

Press your left thumb over the hole
underneath the recorder.
Cover the top hole nearest your mouth
with your first finger.

Put your right thumb under the recorder
opposite the fourth hole.
This helps to hold the recorder.
Look at the picture to help you.

Do not move your fingers.
Now you are ready to play your first note.

Beginning to play

Put the tip of your recorder between your lips.
Do not let it touch your teeth.

Blow gently into the recorder by saying "tu".
It should make a sound called **note B**.

Play note B several times.
Remember to say "tu" each time you play the note.
This is called **tonguing**.

Be careful. Only your left thumb and first finger
should cover holes.

note B

Hold your recorder like you did before.
Only your left thumb and first finger should cover holes.

Play note B four times.
Remember to say "tu" each time.
Make each note sound for the same time.

tu tu tu tu

Diagrams like the one on the right show the fingering for each note.
A black circle shows that you should cover this hole.

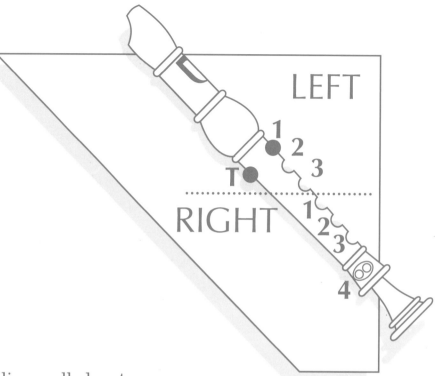

We write musical notes on a set of 5 lines called a **stave**.
Here is note B written four times on the stave.

The sign ♪ at the beginning of each stave is called a **treble clef**.
Play note B again four times.
Check your fingers are in the right place.

note B

Say the words to this song.
Clap in time with the words as you say them.
See how some words last longer than others.

Play the tune on your recorder.
Use note B.
Make the notes match the pattern of the words.

LEFT

RIGHT

Lit - tle   fly,   such   a   clown,

Al-ways   walk-ing   up-side   down.

4

Say and clap the words to this song.
Now play the tune using note B.

or   This note is called a **crotchet** or quarter note.

or   These notes are called **quavers** or eighth notes.

A crotchet lasts twice as long as a quaver.

No   more   milk   to - day.

We have   some from   Thurs - day.

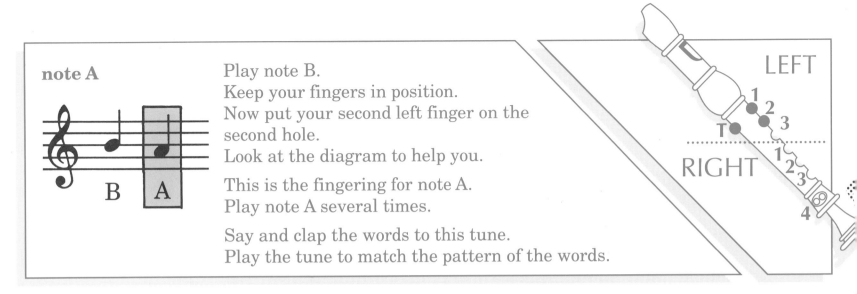

note A

Play note B.
Keep your fingers in position.
Now put your second left finger on the second hole.
Look at the diagram to help you.

This is the fingering for note A.
Play note A several times.

Say and clap the words to this tune.
Play the tune to match the pattern of the words.

Traffic Jam

Lit - tle   bird   in   the   sky,

Fly - ing   free,   fly - ing   high.

Say and clap the words before you play this tune.
Which note is used first on this page?

When you can play this tune, go back to page 6.

Play both tunes, one after the other.
This makes a long tune.

Can you see just where I am,

Stuck, in a traf-fic jam?

Caterpillar bye-bye

Say and clap the words, then play the tune.
Be careful not to hurry the last two notes.

Repeat sign

This tells you to play all
the music before the
sign twice.
Then you can go on.

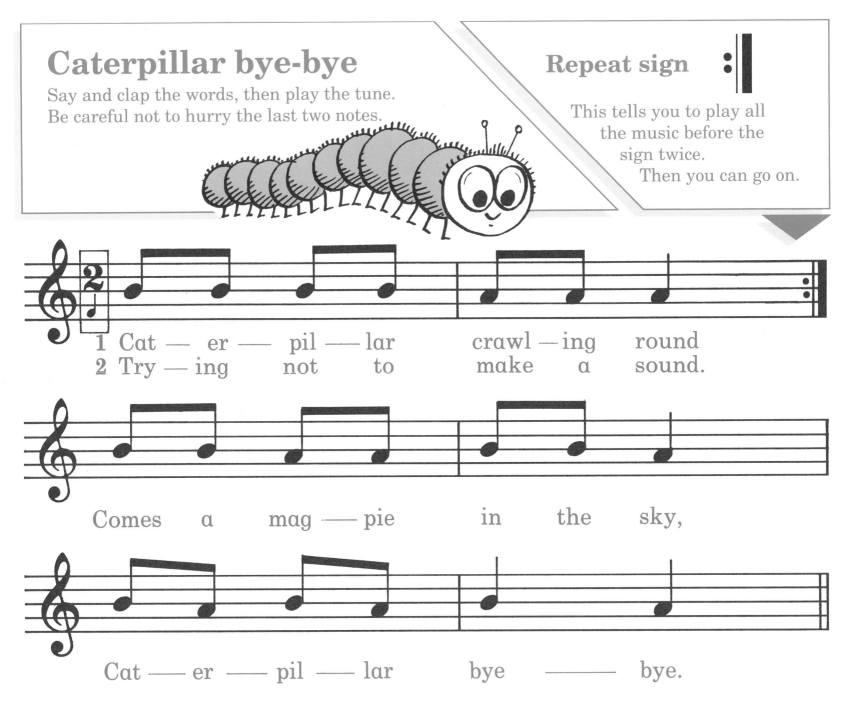

1 Cat — er — pil — lar   crawl — ing   round
2 Try — ing   not   to   make   a   sound.

Comes   a   mag — pie   in   the   sky,

Cat — er — pil — lar   bye — bye.

8

Rhythm Game

Here are parts of some of the tunes you have learned.

Can you play them one at a time?

If you need help, turn back to the tunes.

1  (page 4)

2  (page 8)

Now you can play a game with some friends.
Play either **number 1** or **number 2**.
Can your friends guess which number you played?
Let someone else play one.
Can you guess which one it was?

3  (page 5)

Play the game again using **number 2** and **number 3**.
Now make the game harder by choosing from all three tunes.

note G

Play note A.
Keep your fingers in position.
Now put your third left finger on
the third hole.
Look at the diagram to help you.

This is the fingering for note G. Play it.

Say and clap the words of the first line.
Now play the music of the first line.
Do this for line 2 and line 3.
Join them together and play the whole song.

LEFT

RIGHT

Joe, Joe

© JCP

Joe,   Joe,   stumped his toe,   on the way to   Mex-i-co.

Com-ing back he   hurt his back,   slid-ing on the   rail-road track.

When at home he   broke a bone,   talk-ing on the   tel-e-phone.

10

Gypsy Dance

Count and clap each line of the tune before you play it.
Use the numbers printed above the stave.
Which line has a repeat sign?

For extra tunes using the notes and rhythms met so far,
see 'Recorder from the Beginning' Tune Book 1, page 4.

© JCP

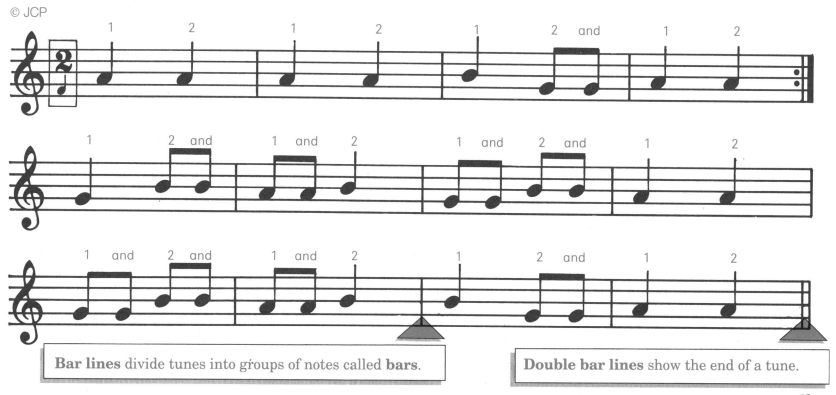

Bar lines divide tunes into groups of notes called **bars**.

Double bar lines show the end of a tune.

Bus Driver

Look at this sign $\boxed{\frac{2}{4}}$ at the beginning of the tune.

It tells us to make each bar last for two **beats**.

This tune uses a new
note which looks like this: ♩

It is called a **minim** or half note.
A minim lasts as long as two crotchets.

Say and clap the words, then play the tune.
To clap a minim say "clap-press" (and do it!)
This takes the time of two beats.

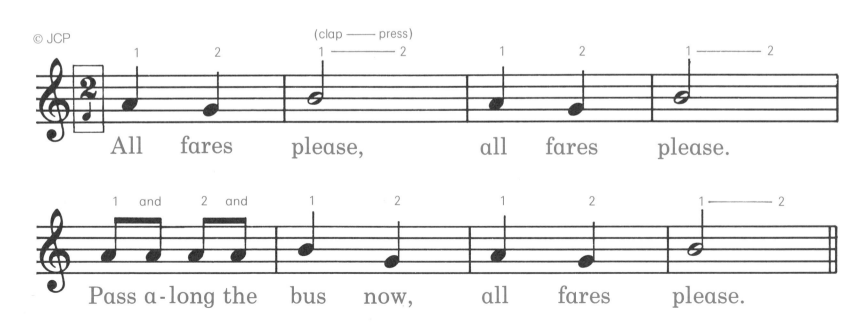

All fares please, all fares please.

Pass a-long the bus now, all fares please.

Traffic Lights

Tongue each note (say "tu")
when you play this tune.

Ask an adult to accompany you.
They can use piano or guitar.
Or your friends can use chime-bars.

All the music is in the Teacher's Book.
Or you can play along with the cassette
accompaniment.

'Stop' says the red light, 'Go' says the green,

'Wait' says the am-ber light, winking in be - tween.

Hot Cross Buns

This tune has four beats in each bar.
What tells us this?
Count and clap before you play the tune.

Sometimes quavers (eighth notes)
are joined together in twos:

Sometimes they are joined together in fours:
They are both played exactly the same.

Hot   cross   buns!   Hot   cross   buns!

One a pen-ny,   two a pen-ny,   hot   cross   buns!

For extra tunes using the notes and rhythms met so far, see 'Recorder from the Beginning' Tune Book 1, pages 5 and 6.

Who's that yonder ?

This tune has a new sign in it:

It means make no sound for one beat:
It is called a **crotchet rest** or quarter note rest.

Count, clap and play this exercise.
Then play the tune.

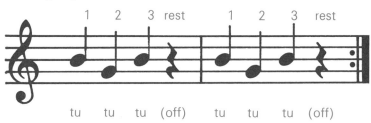

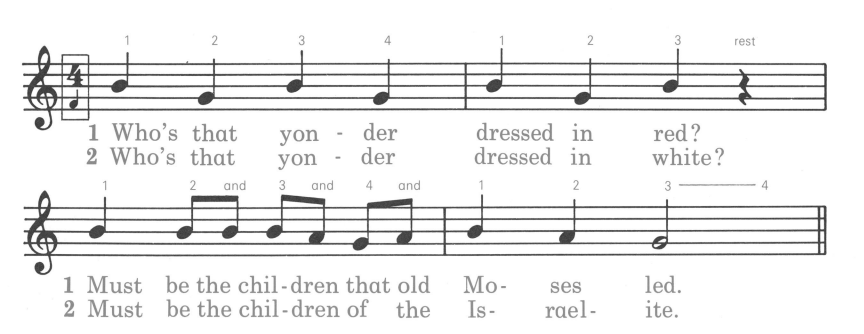

1 Who's that yon - der dressed in red?
2 Who's that yon - der dressed in white?

1 Must be the chil-dren that old Mo - ses led.
2 Must be the chil-dren of the Is - rael- ite.

Here is a tune with three beats in each bar.

Each line ends with a dotted note 𝅗𝅥. worth three beats.

Count and play the tune.

Now read the explanation at the bottom of this page.

Kites

High in the sky the kites all fly.

Don't lose the string, or "Kite, good - bye!"

A dot after a note tells us to add half the value of the note. 𝅗𝅥. = 𝅗𝅥 + ♩

3 = 2 + 1

So 𝅗𝅥. lasts for **3** beats. To clap 𝅗𝅥. go "clap-press-press".

16

This sign ✔ shows you where to take a breath.
Only take breaths at breathing places marked ✔

When you can play this tune, go back to page 16.
Join both tunes together to make one long tune.

Gliding

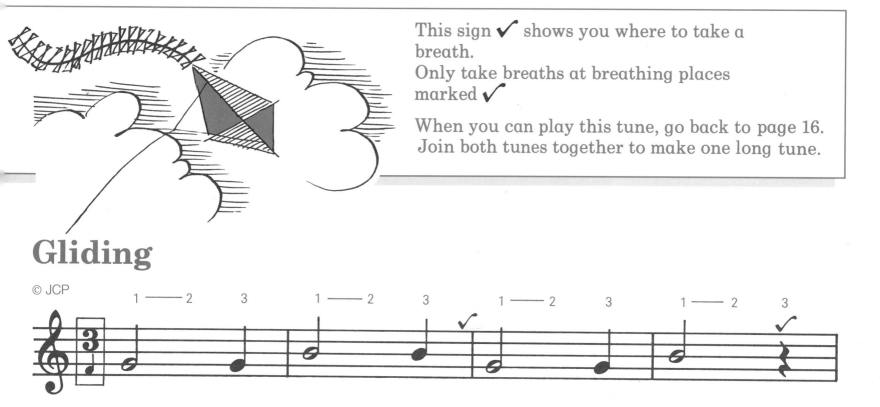

Ask an adult to accompany you.
They can use piano or guitar.
Or your friends can use chime-bars.
All the music is in the Teacher's Book.
Or you can play along with the cassette accompaniment.

For extra tunes using the notes and rhythms met so far, see 'Recorder from the Beginning' Tune Book 1, page 7.

note E

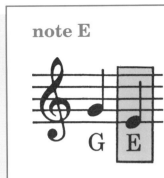

G E

Play note G. Keep your fingers in position.

Now put the first and second fingers of your right hand on the next two holes. Look at the diagram to help you.

This is the fingering for note E. Play it.

Now play the last two bars of the tune. Then play all the tune.

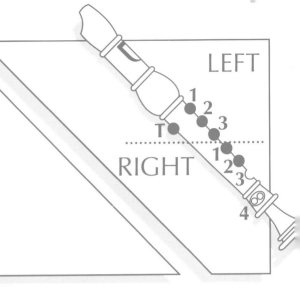

LEFT

RIGHT

Elephants (Not too fast!)

© JCP

Hump, wump, dump, chump

El - eph - ants walk with an aw — ful bump.

group 1

When you can play this tune well, divide into two groups.
One group plays "awful bump" (the last two bars) again and again.
This is called an **ostinato** accompaniment.

The other group plays the tune.
Someone must count, "1–2–3" so that both groups begin together.

Repeat the tune and the groups change parts.

18

Indian Warrior

Say and clap the words, then play the tune.

I'm an In — dian war-ri-or, war-ri-or,

Big chief In — dian war-ri-or, war-ri-or

Hi ho! Hi ho!

Hi Hi, Hi ho!

For extra tunes, see 'Recorder from the Beginning' Tune Book 1, page 8.

A New Rhythm

Count and clap this short tune.
Then play it.

Here is the tune again, with one difference.
This time it uses the **tie** sign ⌣
When two notes are tied together, do not
play the second note.
Hold the first note for the value of both
notes added together.
It makes a longer sound.
Count and clap **tune 2**, then play it.
Remember to hold the tied note.

Tune 3 is another way of writing **tune 2**.
Tune 3 uses a quarter note (crotchet) in
place of two eighth notes (quavers).
We can do this because the eighth notes
were tied together.

Play **tune 3**.
Make it sound exactly the same as **tune 2**.

"Skateboard Ride" on page 21 begins with
tune 3.
Can you find **tune 3** anywhere else in
"Skateboard Ride"?

Play the whole "Ride".

Skateboard Ride

The tune on the next page also uses tied notes. Here they are to practise before you play the tune. Count and clap, then play this line.

Count and clap, then play. Remember to hold the tied note.

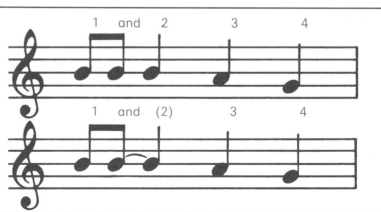

Chicka Hanka – a 'blues' tune

This tune uses two new signs.
Both are worth four beats.

O is called a **semibreve** or whole note.
It keeps sounding for four beats.

Practise the first line
before you play the whole tune.

is called a **semibreve rest** or whole note rest.
It means silence, or rest, for four beats.

For extra tunes using the notes and rhythms met so far, see 'Recorder from the Beginning' Tune Book 1, pages 9 to 11.

* **Think** these words, but do not play them.
They will help you to keep time.

Fandango – a Spanish dance

Can you find any bars which are the same as each other?
Which line is the same as line 2?

Now play the tune.

When you can play the tune well, use this rhythm **ostinato**
(repeating pattern) to make an accompaniment.
Count and clap it. Try saying the words to help you.
Then divide into two groups.
Group 1 plays the rhythm ostinato on tambourine or claves.
Group 2 plays the tune on their recorders. Then change round.

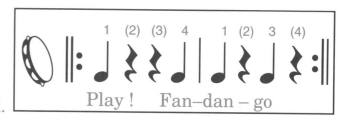

note D

Play note E. Keep your fingers in position.
Now put the third finger of your right hand on the next hole.
Use the diagram to help you.

This is the fingering for note D. Play it.

LEFT

RIGHT

Tied notes
Remember (page 20) that when two notes are tied we do not play the second note.

We add its value to the first note. Play both these tunes and listen to the difference.

Chatter with the Angels

Chatter with the an-gels   soon in the morn-ing,   Chatter with the an-gels   in that land. join that band.

I   hope to join that band and   chatter with the an-gels   all day long.

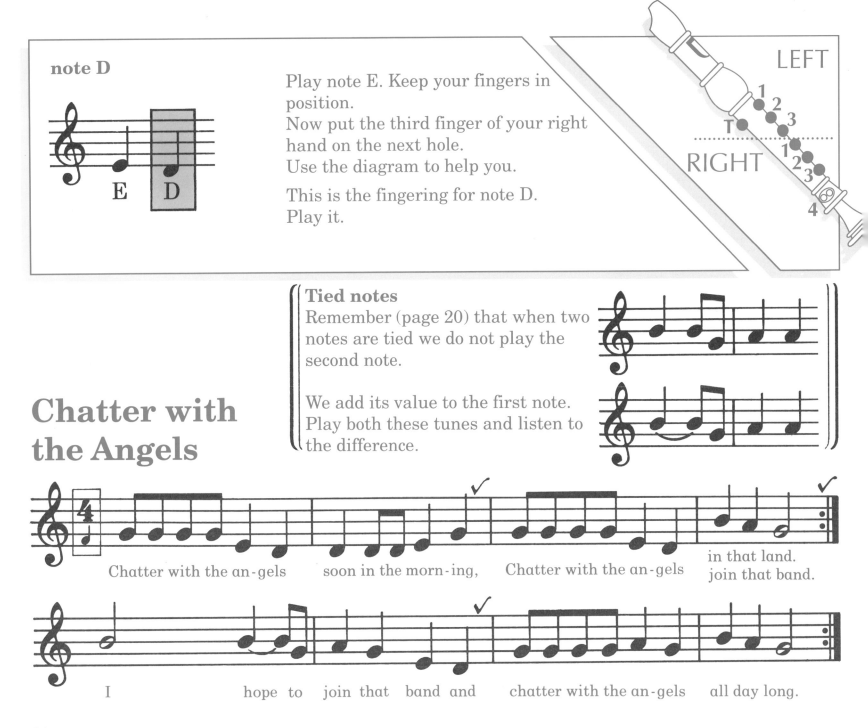

Mocking Bird

Here are two tunes to play.
The second one uses all the notes you know.

Hush lit-tle ba- by   don't say a word,   Mammy's going to buy   you a   mock-ing bird.

If   that   mock-ing   bird won't   sing,   Mammy's going to buy   you a   dia-mond ring.

The Swapping Song

When I was   a   lit-tle boy I   lived   by my-self   And

all the bread and cheese I   got   I   kept up-on   a   shelf——   Wing wong   wad-dle   to my

jack   straw   sad-dle,   To   my   John   fair   fad-dle, to my   long   ways   home.

For extra tunes, see 'Recorder from the Beginning' Tune Book 1, pages 12 and 13.

25

The next tune uses some **slurred** notes.
The sign is a curved line, rather like a tie sign.
But a slur sign joins different notes.
To play two notes which are slurred together tongue the first note but not the second.
Keep blowing, but change fingering to make the second note.
The slur joins different notes together smoothly.
Be careful not to mix up slurred notes and tied notes.
Practise these slurs using these parts of the tune.

tongue slur   t ———   t ——— t   t ——— t

Karen's Waltz

Now play "Adele's Waltz".
Be careful with the slurs.
When you can play all the tune without any mistakes, you may read the special upside-down message!

For another tune using the same slurred notes, see 'Recorder from the Beginning' Tune Book 1, page 14.

Karen and Adele are twin sisters. Adele's Waltz is a special tune that fits with Karen's Waltz.
Divide into two groups and play both tunes at the same time.
Someone must count 1-2-3 so that both groups start exactly together.
When one tune fits with another tune, we call the extra tune a **descant.**

Adele's Waltz

Old MacDonald

Old Mac-Don-ald had a farm, E I E I Oh! And

on that farm he had some chicks E I E I Oh! With a

chick-chick here and a chick-chick there, Here a chick, there a chick, ev-'ry where a chick-chick.

Old Mac-Don-ald had a farm, E I E I Oh! And Oh!

2 turkeys (gobble-gobble)
3 pigs (grunt-grunt)
4 sheep (baa-baa)
5 cows (moo-moo)

Rhythm Game

Here are some bars from the tune "Old MacDonald".
Practise each bar, and then choose one to play to your friends.
Can your friends guess which bar you played?

The person who guessed the right bar has the next turn.

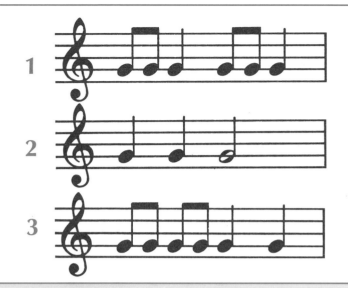

Pitch Game (Pitch means whether a note is high or low.)

Here are some more bars from "Old MacDonald".
Practise them so that you can play them without mistakes.
Listen very carefully while someone plays tune **1** or **2**.
Which was it?
How could you tell which bar was played?
(Don't watch fingers!)

Which is it?
1 or **2**?

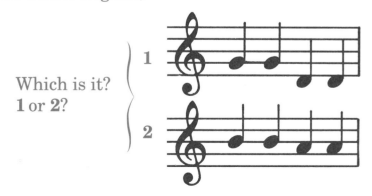

Now try with **3** and **4**.

Which is it?
3 or **4**?

Staccato notes

We have already seen notes with a dot after them.

♩. is a dotted minim (or dotted half-note).

A dot after a note makes the note half as long again.

Now we are going to play notes with a dot above or below them
This tells us to play the notes **staccato**, or cut off short.
To do this, say "tut" instead of "tu".

Play these.

Now see if you can play staccato–smoothly–staccato–smoothly.
Be careful to give full value to notes which are not staccato.

The tune on the next page uses staccato notes and slurs.
Here they are to practise.

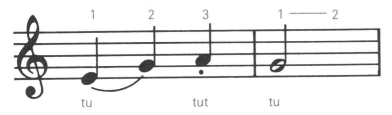

Now find them in the tune and play them again.

For another tune using staccato notes, see 'Recorder from the Beginning' Tune Book 1, page 14.

Dear Liza

Most of this tune is similar to the first line.

Notice that the tune begins on count 3.
Say 1–2 and begin to play on 3.

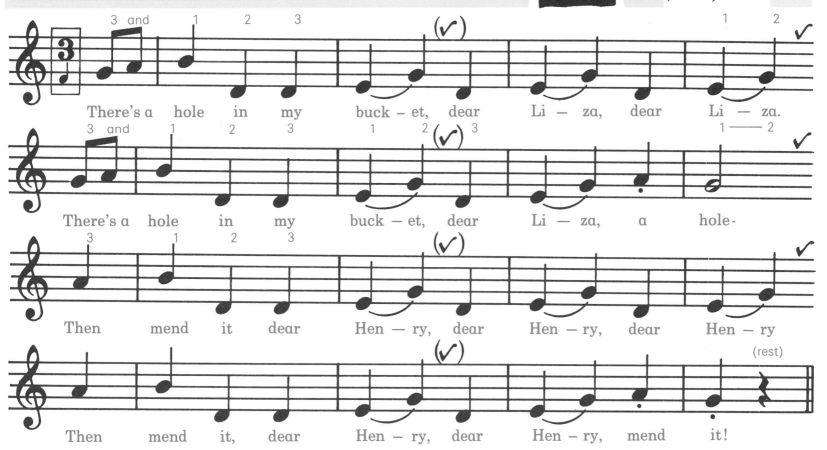

note C' (upper C)

A C'

The next note we will learn is called C' (upper C).
First play note A, then take off your left first finger.
Keep your second finger and thumb covering the holes.
Look at the diagram to help you.

This is note C' (upper C). Play it.

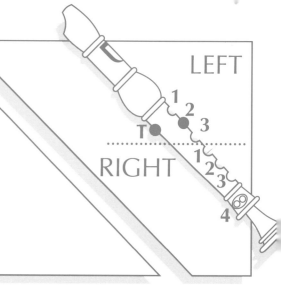

LEFT

RIGHT

Tadpoles

Ten   lit-tle   tad —— poles   Play-ing   in   a   pool.

'Come'   said the   wat-er   rat,   'Come a — long   to   school.

Come and say your   ta —— bles,   Sit-ting   in   a   row'   And

all the   lit-tle   tad — poles,   said   'No,   No,   No!'

Play and sing a round, Little Bell

For extra tunes and four duets, see 'Recorder from the Beginning' Tune Book 1, pages 16 to 23.

The next tune begins with the end of a bar.

Can you play this tune twice without stopping at all?

When you can, divide into two groups and play the tune as a **round**.

One group starts. When they have played the first four notes, the other group starts to play from the beginning. Each group should stop when they have played the whole tune twice.

Class Activities

A group of **singers** can be Group 1, with all the recorder players as Group 2.

You can add an ostinato accompaniment (repeating pattern) on a xylophone, a glockenspiel or chime bars. The ostinato is only four notes long and easy to learn.

Then try a class performance with singers, recorders and ostinato players. Begin like this.

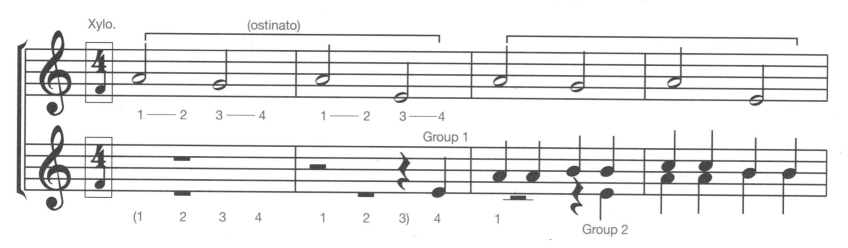

More About Rhythm

The "Lament" on page 35 uses a new way of writing the rhythm
You played this rhythm in "Tadpoles" on page 32.
The exercises below show both ways of writing this rhythm.

Clap and count then play.
Be careful with the staccato notes.

1

Remember when two notes are tied you do
not play the second note.
Add its value to the first note.

2

Here is another way to write the same
rhythm.
The dot after the note makes the note half
as long again.
2 and **3** should sound exactly the same.

3

Now you have learned part of line 3 of "Lament".
Can you find three other places in the tune which use the same rhythm,
but with different notes?
Play them.

34

Lament

Notice that the tune begins on count 4.
Say 1–2–3 and begin to play on 4.
Later someone can add a rhythm **ostinato**.
Play it on claves or tambourine.

Fairly slowly

© JCP

35

Loch Morlich

Slowly, with a lilt

When you can play this tune without mistakes, try the descant on the next page.

Later, you and your friends could play both tunes at once.

Count 1–2–3 to help you to begin together.

For more duets and other tunes using the notes and rhythms from this book, see 'Recorder from the Beginning' Tune Book 1, pages 22 to 29.

Descant to **Loch Morlich**

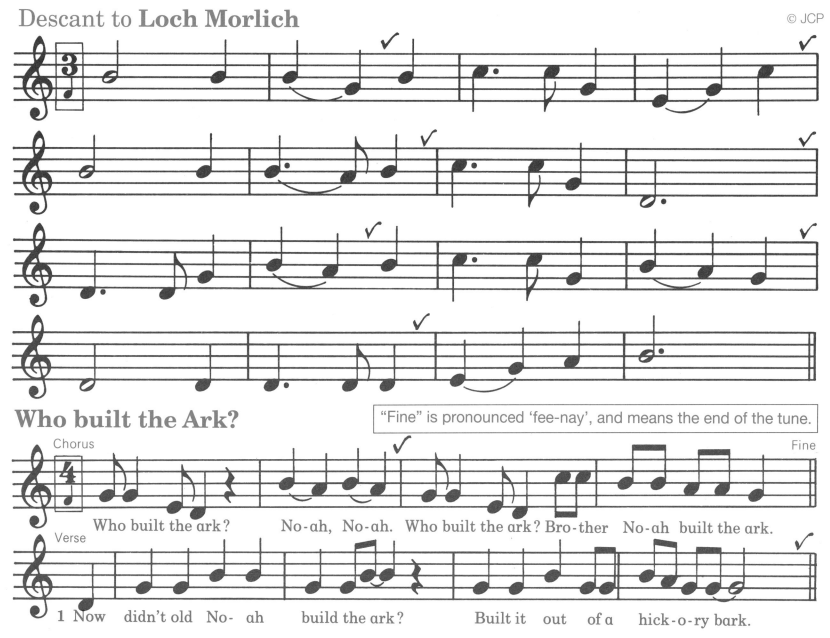

Who built the Ark?

"Fine" is pronounced 'fee-nay', and means the end of the tune.

Chorus

Who built the ark? No-ah, No-ah. Who built the ark? Bro-ther No-ah built the ark.

Verse

1 Now didn't old No-ah build the ark? Built it out of a hick-o-ry bark.

2 He built it long, both wide and tall, Plenty of room for one and all.

3 Now in came the animals two by two, Hip-po-pota-mus and kan-ga-roo.

Making up tunes using notes we know

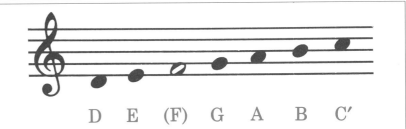

D E (F) G A B C'

For more tune writing see 'Recorder from the Beginning'
Tune Book 1, pages 30 and 31.

 Say the words and clap the rhythm of **tune 1**. Then play it.

Tune 1

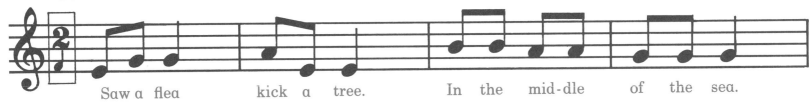

Saw a flea   kick a tree.   In the mid-dle   of the sea.

Now say the words and clap the rhythm of **tune 2**.
Clap the rhythm of the first part again, saying the words quietly.

Tune 2

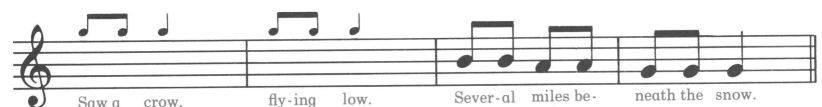

Saw a crow,   fly-ing low.   Sever-al miles be-   neath the snow.

Make up a little tune on your recorder.
Make it fit the words you clapped.
Start with any note you choose.
Try again, until you like your tune.

Play your tune, and finish it off with the rest of **tune 2**.
You could write out the whole tune on manuscript paper.

B Make up an ending for **tune 3**.

First play the beginning which is printed below.

Now make up a tune to fit the rest of the words.

Say the words and clap the rhythm to help you.

Tune 3

Have some fun.

Play the first part of **tune 3** with some friends.

Choose one person to keep on playing and make up an ending.

Then let someone else have a try.

C See if you can make up all of **tune 4**. Use the words to give you the rhythm.

You might need to write down the notes to help you remember your tune.

Then you can play **tunes 4** and **5** straight after each other.

Now can you play all the tunes without stopping?

Tune 4

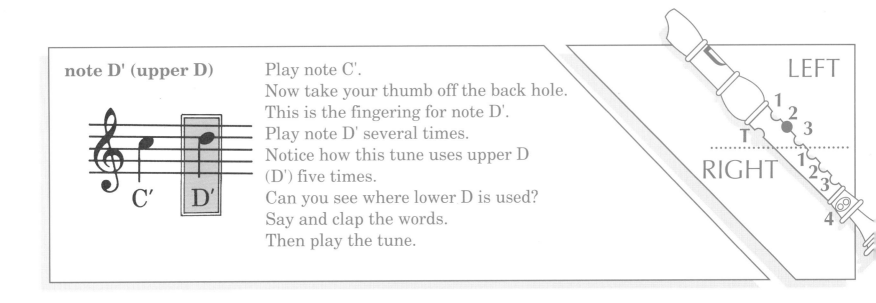

note D' (upper D)

C'   D'

Play note C'.
Now take your thumb off the back hole.
This is the fingering for note D'.
Play note D' several times.
Notice how this tune uses upper D
(D') five times.
Can you see where lower D is used?
Say and clap the words.
Then play the tune.

LEFT

RIGHT

Way down South

© JCP (Tune)

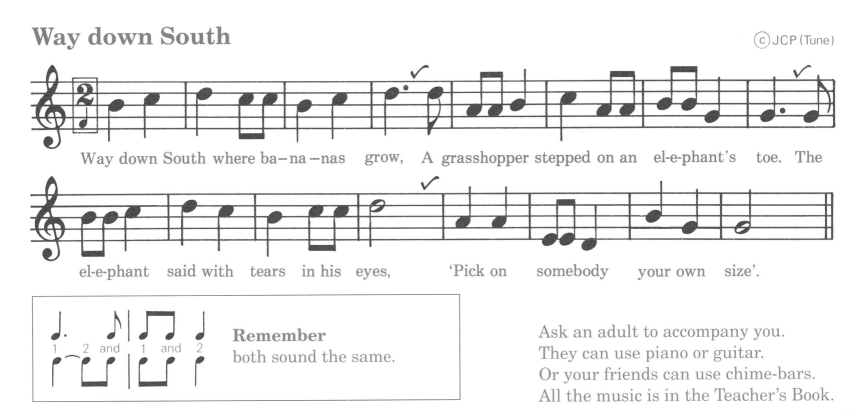

Way down South where ba-na-nas grow, A grasshopper stepped on an el-e-phant's toe. The

el-e-phant said with tears in his eyes, 'Pick on somebody your own size'.

Remember
both sound the same.

Ask an adult to accompany you.
They can use piano or guitar.
Or your friends can use chime-bars.
All the music is in the Teacher's Book.

Ten in the bed

This tune begins with the end of a bar. To begin, count 1–2–3 and play on count 4.

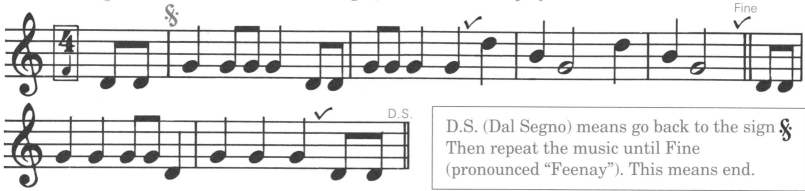

D.S. (Dal Segno) means go back to the sign 𝄋
Then repeat the music until Fine
(pronounced "Feenay"). This means end.

London's burning   Count 1–2 and play on count 3.

Class Activity

When you know this tune well, you can play it as a **Round** in 2, 3 or 4 parts. Or some **Singers** can be Group 1 (and 3) with Recorders as Group 2 (and 4).

Ostinato accompaniment. You can use the first or last phrase of the round as an ostinato accompaniment (repeating pattern). Play it on xylophone or chime bars. Let the ostinato begin first before the singers and recorders join in with the round. Later try both ostinati together.

Amazing Grace
Remember to tongue–slur where a curved line joins **different** notes (slurred).

A —ma——zing grace, how sweet the sound, That saved a wretch like me———. I

once —— was lost, but now—— I'm found, Was blind, but now I see————.

Over the sea to Skye

D.C. (Da Capo) means go back to the beginning, and repeat until Fine.

Fais Dodo (French Lullaby)

Rhythm Game

Here are some parts out of the tunes on page 4.
See if you can play them one at a time.
All have 3 counts in each bar.

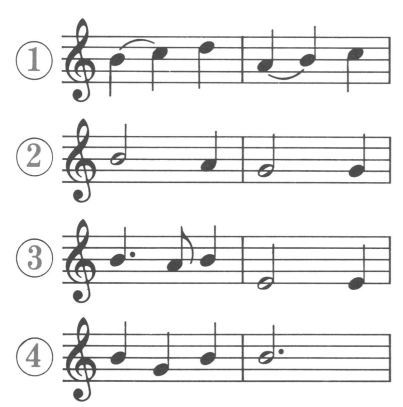

For extra tunes and a duet using the notes and rhythms met so far, see 'Recorder from the Beginning' Tune Book 2, pages 4 to 7.

Now play the game with some friends.
Cover up **numbers 3** and **4** before you begin.
Play either **number 1** or **number 2**.
See if your friends can guess which one you played.
Then let someone else play one, and you all guess again.

Later use **numbers 3** and **4** instead.
Cover up **1** and **2**.
Make the game harder: cover up **number 1**
or **4** only. Choose from the other three!

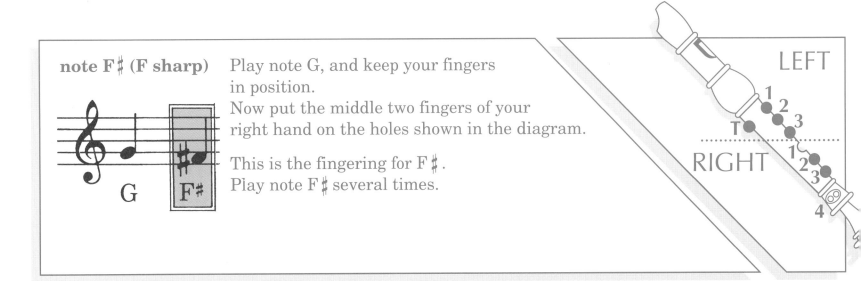

note F♯ (F sharp)

G   F♯

Play note G, and keep your fingers in position.
Now put the middle two fingers of your right hand on the holes shown in the diagram.

This is the fingering for F♯.
Play note F♯ several times.

LEFT

RIGHT

Notice the sharp sign ♯ in front of the note.
This makes it a special note. Later we will
learn to play F natural, which uses different fingering.

Zulu Lullaby

Fine

1   2   3 – 4

1 and 2 and   3 and 4

D.C.

44

Some tunes use note F♯ (F sharp) instead of note F all the way through. Then, instead of writing the sharp sign (♯) in front of each note F, we place it at the beginning of the stave on the top line, which is also note F.

This turns every F into F♯, including those written in the bottom space.

Sharp (♯) or flat (♭) signs placed at the beginning of a stave are called the **Key Signature**.

Sinner Man

Oh, sinner man, where you gon-na run to? Oh, sinner man, where you gon-na run to?

Oh, sin-ner man, where you gon-na run to? All on that day ————.

Tallis's Canon begins at the end of a bar.

Count 1–2–3 and start to play on count 4. When you know the tune well, play it as a proper Canon.

Divide into two groups.
Group 1 begins.
When they reach letter A on the music, Group 2 begins playing from the beginning.

Cradle Song

This tune begins at the end of a bar.
Count 1–2 and play on count 3.
Notice the sharp sign.

Winter Journey

Take special care with
the slurs in this piece.

Time Signatures

The number on the stave just before the first note of a tune is called the Time Signature.

This tells us how many "conductor's beats" there are in each bar.
If we do as the Time Signature tells us, we can conduct the band for any tune.

Try to "conduct" a tune whilst someone plays it.
First practise your conducting using the shapes given here.
Count the beats as you conduct them.

When you are ready, turn back to the full tune.
Always count and conduct for one bar before the players join in.
This helps them to begin together.
Use a pencil for a baton!

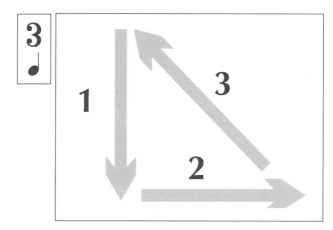

Sinner Man (Page 7)

Oh, sinner man, where you gon-na run to?

Fais Dodo (Page 4)

1 – 2 3   1 – 2 3   1   2   3   1 – 2 3

Pokare Kare Maori song

This song is about some Maoris who are on a hunting trip, away from their families.

The tune and descant both use exactly the same rhythm. When you are playing in two parts, always listen carefully.

Are you playing in time together?

Is your part louder than the other?

It shouldn't be!

Descant

More about **Time Signatures**

The shape for conducting four beats in a bar is hard to remember.
Think of a sailing ship.

1	Down	(down the mast)
2	Back	(to the back of the boat)
3	Front	(to the front of the boat)
4	Up	(up the sail)

Count four beats in a bar and practise conducting this shape.

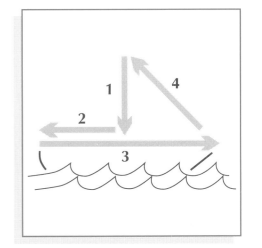

Later you can take turns to conduct "Good King Wenceslas", whilst others play the tune.
Take care to keep conducting and counting during the long notes.

Good King Wenceslas

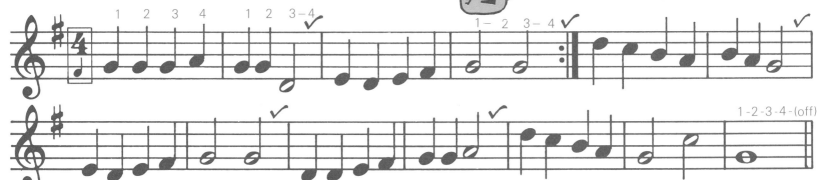

50

Another tune to play and then conduct.
Remember the Time Signature tells us how many
conductor's beats there are in each full bar, not
how many notes there are.

For extra tunes and a duet using the notes and
rhythms met so far, see 'Recorder from the
Beginning' Tune Book 2, pages 8 to 11.

Down in Bethlehem

© JH

(Verse) Little baby wrapped in white, Sleeping in the candle light, Mary watching thro'the night, Down in Bethlehem.

(Chorus) Far a—way, Far a—way, Jesus came to earth on Christ-mas Day.

Not all tunes start on the strong beat
at the beginning of a bar.
Some start on a weak beat at the end
of a bar. This is called an **anacrusis**.

Then we must count the rest of the bar
before we begin.
Turn back and play these tunes again,
counting the beats before you begin.

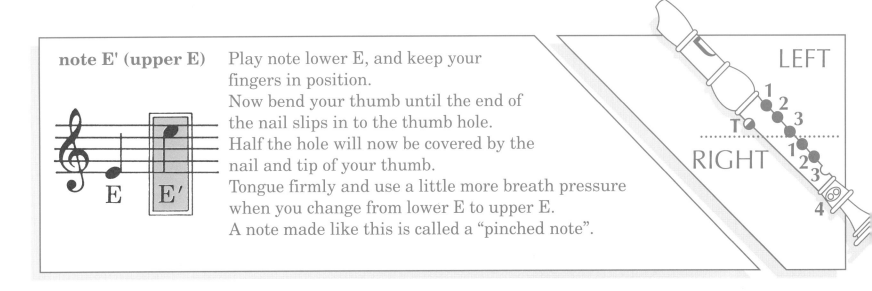

note E′ (upper E) Play note lower E, and keep your fingers in position.
Now bend your thumb until the end of the nail slips in to the thumb hole.
Half the hole will now be covered by the nail and tip of your thumb.
Tongue firmly and use a little more breath pressure when you change from lower E to upper E.
A note made like this is called a "pinched note".

Before learning the tune, practise playing from E′ to D′.
Where is this used in the tune?

Old Abram Brown

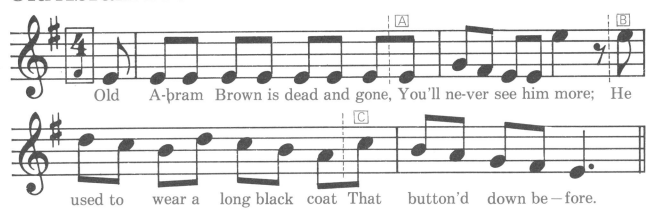

Old A-bram Brown is dead and gone, You'll ne-ver see him more; He used to wear a long black coat That button'd down be—fore.

This is a **round** that will fit in two, three or four parts.
Letters A , B and C show where the starting points are.

52

My Bonnie lies over the ocean

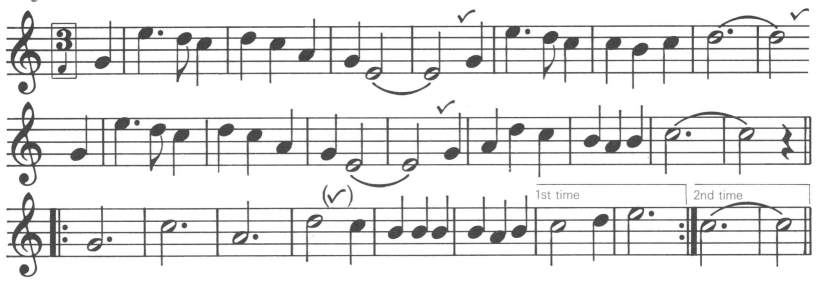

French Carol

For eight duets and some carols using the notes and rhythms met so far, see 'Recorder from the Beginning' Tune Book 2, pages 12 to 20.

An optional second part is given to accompany the chorus. The **tune** notes have stems up (♩) and the **accompaniment** notes have stems down (♩).

Now all the forests are at rest (Old German hymn)

In the next tune, notice how the first two bars of lines 1 and 2 are the same.

Is the second half of line 2 used anywhere else?

Remember that a dot above or below a note  makes the note **staccato**, or cut off short.

To play staccato say 'tut'.

When you play the tune, be careful to tongue the staccato and slurred notes correctly.

The Lord Mayor's Parade

The next song uses two new rhythm patterns, ♪♫ and ♫♪

First, say the words and clap the rhythms of (a) and (b).

(a)

That is what I heard her say

(b)

Grandma Grunts said a curious thing

In line (b) two **semi-quavers** or sixteenth notes take the place of one **quaver** or eighth note

Grandma Grunts

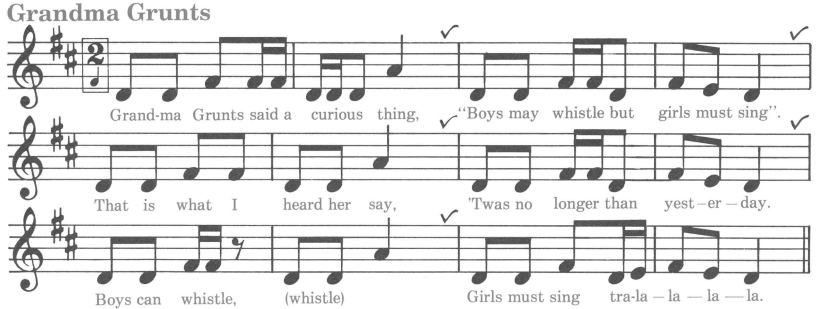

Grand-ma Grunts said a curious thing, "Boys may whistle but girls must sing".

That is what I heard her say, 'Twas no longer than yest–er—day.

Boys can whistle, (whistle) Girls must sing tra-la—la—la—la.

Skip to my Lou

Lou,   lou,   skip   to my lou,   Lou,   lou,   skip   to my lou,

Lou,   lou,   skip   to my lou,   skip   to my   lou   my   dar——ling.

The next tune (on page 20) uses two new rhythms, ♩♩♩♩ and ♩. ♩
Can you find them in the tune? (Turn over to look, then read on here.)
See how four semiquavers (sixteenth notes) take the time of the first crotchet (quarter note) beat.
Try to clap all the first bar as you say the words.

Here is an exercise to help you learn the other new rhythm.

First play this: (a)

Play again but hold on the tied note: (b)

Here is another way to write (b).
The dot after a note makes the note half as
long again, so (b) and (c) should sound
exactly the same.   (c)

Little Red Wagon

Riding up and down in the little red wag-on, Riding up and down in the little red wag-on,

Riding up and down in the little red wag-on, Won't you be my dar———ling?

Class Activity

Now you can have some fun!

The tunes of 'Skip to my Lou' and 'Little Red Wagon' will fit together. Split up into two groups and try to play both tunes at the same time!

Someone must count 1–2 so that you all begin together.

Singers

A group of singers can perform one tune whilst recorders play the other tune. Then change over.

The Teacher's Book has suggestions for an easy accompaniment that will fit either tune or both tunes together. Or you can use the cassette accompaniment.

Both these tunes begin with the end of a bar.
Count 1–2 and play on count 3.

Kum ba ya

Kum ba ya my Lord, Kum ba ya —, Kum ba ya my Lord, Kum ba ya,

Kum ba ya my Lord, Kum ba ya, O Lord —— Kum ba ya.

Clementine

In a ca—vern, in a can—yon, Ex-ca-vat——ing for a mine,

Lived a min—er, for—ty nin——er, And his daugh——ter Clem-en—tine.

Chorus (same tune)
Oh, my darling, Oh, my darling,
Oh, my darling Clementine!
You are lost and gone forever,
Dreadful sorry, Clementine.

Anacrusis
An incomplete bar at the beginning of a tune is
called an **anacrusis**. Then the music starts on a
weak beat instead of a strong one. Notice that the
last bar of the tune is also incomplete. Add this to
the anacrusis and it makes a full bar.

More tunes that use E' (upper E)

For a duet and an extra tune see 'Recorder from the Beginning' Tune Book 2, page 21.

Ten Green Bottles

Remember both sound the same. (See Book 1 page 20.)

Missa Ram Goat

Land of the silver birch

Kalinka

 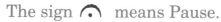

Cossack Dance

is a minim (half note) rest worth two beats.

©JCP

61

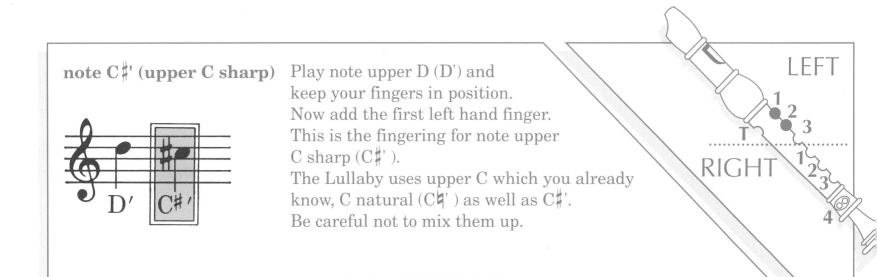

note C#' (upper C sharp)

Play note upper D (D') and keep your fingers in position. Now add the first left hand finger. This is the fingering for note upper C sharp (C#').

The Lullaby uses upper C which you already know, C natural (C♮') as well as C#'. Be careful not to mix them up.

Manx Lullaby

Before you play
"Vilikins", practise these bars
taken from the tune.

Vilikins and his Dinah

repeat only the music shown between repeat signs

The Banks of Sacramento

Ho, boys, ho ——! For Ca—li-for—nia, O! There's
plenty of gold, so . I've been told, On the banks of Sa——cra—men-to.

For two duets and extra tunes see 'Recorder from the Beginning'
Tune Book 2, pages 22 to 25.

Class Activity

Kookaburra is a **round** that will fit in two, three or four parts.
You can use **singers** and an **ostinato** as explained on page 3.

Kook a bur ra sits in an old gum tree, Merry merry king of the bush is he—

Laugh Kook a bur ra, Laugh Kook a bur ra, Gay your life will be ——————

Tzena has an optional second part to accompany the chorus.
The chorus tune has stems up, the accompaniment tune has stems down.

Chorus

A **Mazurka** is a Polish dance,
usually in three sections.
The beginning and end are the same, so we
have used the D.C. sign to tell you when to
go back to the beginning.
Take care to play the slurs properly.

Mazurka

The words of this rhyme will help you to learn some new rhythm patterns that skip along. Say and clap the words, then play the tune.

Incey Wincey Spider

In — cey win — cey spi — der Climb-ing up the wat — er spout.

Down came the rain And washed the spi — der out.

Out came the sun And dried up all the rain, So

In — cey win — cey spi — der Climbed the spout a — gain.

London Bridge

Say and clap, then play. Take care with the quicker notes ♪♪♪ in bar 3 and bar 6.

Lon don Bridge   is   brok —en down,   Dance   over my   Lad — y   Lee.

Lon — don Bridge   is   brok —— en down, With a   gay   Lad ——— y.

Skipping for fun

In the last two tunes you played
all the rhythms you need in this tune.

Haul Away Joe (Shanty)

Way, haul a—way——————, We'll haul a—way the bow——lin'——,

Way, haul a—way——————, We'll haul a—way Joe.

So far all the skipping rhythms we have met have been fast, like "Haul Away Joe".
The words helped us to fit in the notes, or we used two big counts in each bar.
Slower skipping tunes use six little counts in each bar, grouped in threes: ♪♪♪ ♪♪♪
The Time Signature will be 6/8

See how the notes can fit together. Count and clap each line.

Use 1 count for ♪

Use 2 counts for ♩ (= ♫)

Use 3 counts for ♩. (= ♫♪ or ♩♪)

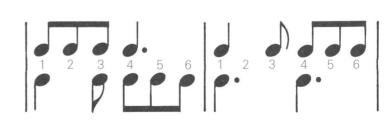

Count and clap each tune before you play it.

What would you do?

©JCP (Tune)

For extra tunes using these rhythms see 'Recorder from the Beginning' Tune Book 2, pages 26 and 27.

What would you do if you had a cow, Who

nev–er said 'Moo' but pre——ferred a 'Bow-wow'. Who

played the guit–ar and lived in a stye, And

put on gol–osh–es to keep her feet dry?

Row, Row, Row your boat (Round) Ideas for **Class Activity** are on page 3.

Row, row, row your boat, Gent—ly down the stream———,

Merr-i-ly, merr-i-ly, merr-i-ly, merr-i-ly, Life is such a dream———.

The first Nowell (Includes C♯')

For more carols, including duets, see 'Recorder from the Beginning' Tune Book 2, pages 14 to 17.

God rest you merry, Gentlemen (Includes E')

Unto us a boy is born

The Child's Carol

A Child this day is born

Repeat for Chorus

The **Tango** is a dance from Argentina,
a country in South America.
A Tango always uses the rhythm
How many times is this rhythm used in the
dance tune here?
Look out for the Upper Es and C sharps.

Tango   Not too fast

For six more duets see 'Recorder from the Beginning'
Tune Book 2, pages 18 to 21 and 23 to 24.

Learn to play the tune first.
Then learn the accompaniment.
Later, you and a friend can play both
parts at once. You can also play along
with the cassette accompaniment.

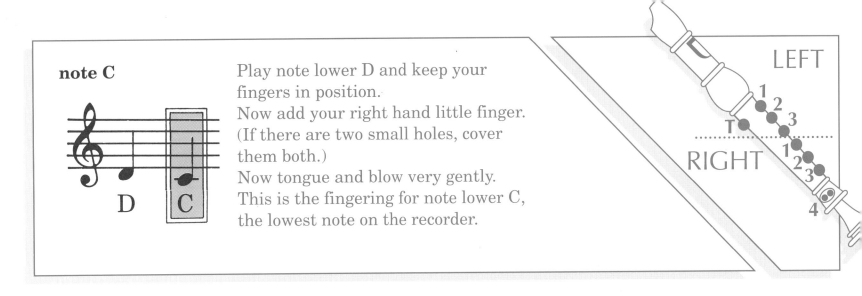

note C

D

C

Play note lower D and keep your fingers in position.
Now add your right hand little finger. (If there are two small holes, cover them both.)
Now tongue and blow very gently.
This is the fingering for note lower C, the lowest note on the recorder.

LEFT

RIGHT

1
2
3
T
1
2
3
4

All the holes on your recorder should be covered. If the note doesn't sound correctly, make sure all your fingers are flat and covering the holes.
Tongue and blow very gently.

Barnyard Song Practise the last bar of the first line before you play the tune.

I had a cat and the cat pleased me,   I fed my cat by yon- der tree.

verse 1

verses 2 – 3

Cat goes   fiddle – i — dee.

Hen goes chinny chuck,   Cat goes   fiddle – i — dee.
Duck goes quack quack,

Here are two more tunes which use lower C.

The fireman's not for me

Old Joe Clark

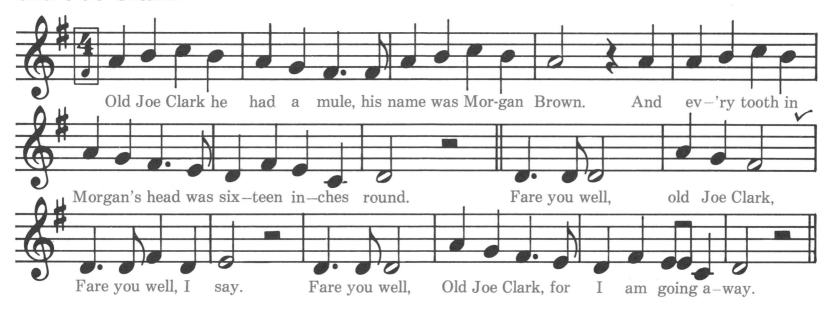

Old Joe Clark he had a mule, his name was Mor-gan Brown. And ev—'ry tooth in

Morgan's head was six—teen in—ches round. Fare you well, old Joe Clark,

Fare you well, I say. Fare you well, Old Joe Clark, for I am going a—way.

Class Activity

Both halves of this tune can be played or sung at the same time. So when you know the tune well, split into two groups.

Singers can be Group 1. They start at A.
Recorders can be Group 2. They start at B.
When Group 2 reach the end they go straight back to A and play up to B again.
Both groups should finish together.

Hollow elm tree

Count 1 – 2 – 3 and play on count 4.

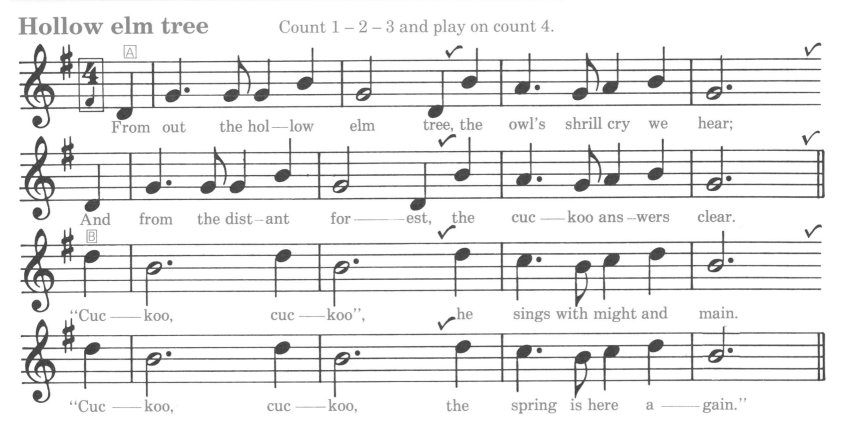

From out the hol—low elm tree, the owl's shrill cry we hear;

And from the dist—ant for——est, the cuc——koo ans—wers clear.

"Cuc——koo, cuc——koo", he sings with might and main.

"Cuc——koo, cuc——koo, the spring is here a——gain."

Li'l Liza Jane

I know a girl that you don't know, Li'l Li——za Jane,

Way down South in Bal—ti——mo', Li'l Li——za Jane.

Oh, E——li——za, li'l Li——za Jane,

Oh, E——li——za, li'l Li——za Jane.

Class Activity

When you can play the song well, you can add two **ostinato** accompaniments. They are made from parts of the tune marked A and B .

You can use xylophone, chime bars or recorders.

Only use ostinato A to begin with.

Play A twice before the tune joins in. Later, try using ostinato B instead.

To use both ostinato parts together, start like a round. Begin with ostinato A .

Then ostinato B joins in.

Both keep playing, then **singers** and/or **recorders** join in with the main tune.

Both these tunes have an **anacrusis**.

They begin with the end of a bar.

Count 1 2 3 4 5 and begin on count 6.

Notice how the first and last bars add together to make one full bar.

It's raining, it's pouring Can you play the second line in one breath?

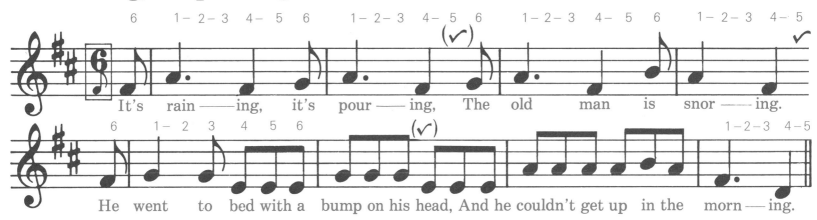

It's rain——ing, it's pour——ing, The old man is snor——ing.

He went to bed with a bump on his head, And he couldn't get up in the morn——ing.

There was a young farmer of Leeds

© JCP (Tune)

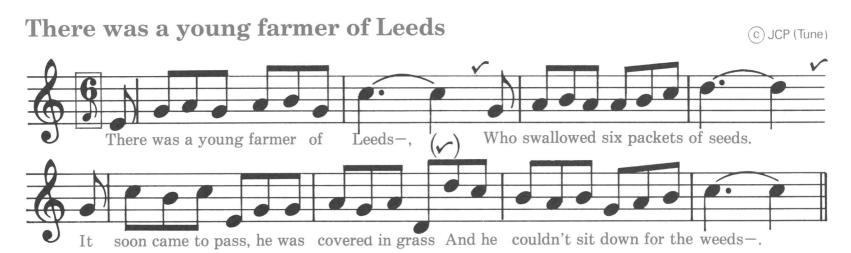

There was a young farmer of Leeds—, Who swallowed six packets of seeds.

It soon came to pass, he was covered in grass And he couldn't sit down for the weeds—.

Scarborough Fair (Includes C♯′ and E′)

One More River (Includes E′)

More use of notes lower C and upper E.

Old Paint

For more tunes using lower C and upper E see 'Recorder from the Beginning' Tune Book 2, pages 28 to 29.

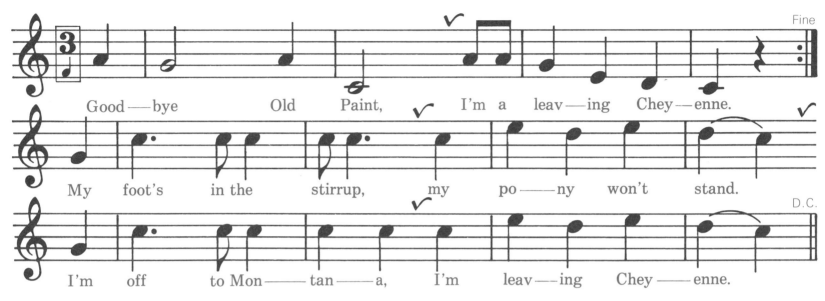

Good — bye Old Paint, I'm a leav — ing Chey — enne.

My foot's in the stirrup, my po — ny won't stand.

I'm off to Mon — tan — a, I'm leav — ing Chey — enne.

Shule Agra

Botany Bay The verse and chorus both use the same tune.

Class Activity see page 3 for help in using singers and players.

I like the flowers Round in 2, 3 or 4 parts

I   like the flow — ers,   I   like   the daff — o –dils,   I   like the moun-tains,

I   like the roll-ing hills.   I   like   the fire ——— side,   when   all the lamps are low,

(Last time only)

Boom-ter-arr-ah,   boom-ter-arr-ah,   boom-ter-arr-ah,   boom-ter-arr-ah,   Boom!

Mango Walk

This tune usually has a **Rumba** accompaniment.
Ask a friend to play the maracas,
using this word pattern to keep the rhythm.

Later, someone else can add claves (or a wooden block,
or rhythm sticks). Count 8 quaver beats in each bar,
and tap on counts ①, ④ and ⑦.

go man-go walk and

① 2 3 ④ 5 6 ⑦ 8

Concert Beguine (Quite slowly)

© JCP

The **Beguine** is a dance from South America. It combines two rhythms. Ask a friend to clap the first rhythm or play it on claves while you play the tune.

Your friend should play the pattern twice as an introduction before you begin. Count the beats aloud. Later another friend can play the second rhythm, using a tambourine. Count aloud and only tap each time you say "and".

To play both rhythms at once, Player 1 begins and after two bars Player 2 joins in. After two more bars the recorders begin the tune.

Tune writing using notes we know

C D E F# G A B C' C#' D' E'

See if you can make up some music to finish off the tune on the next page.
Follow the instructions carefully.

A   Say and clap line 1, then play it.

B   Say the words and clap the rhythm of the first half of line 2.
Now make up some tune on your recorder to fit the words you clapped.
Begin on the notes given.
Keep trying until you like your tune, then write it down.
Now do the same thing again to complete the second line.
End the line on one of the four notes given.

C   Make up line 3 in the same way.
Say and clap the words first.

D   Play the last line. Keep trying different notes to fill in the empty bar until you like the tune.
Then write down the notes.

Two little monkeys

For more tune writing see 'Recorder from the Beginning' Tune Book 2, pages 30 to 31.

Contents

8/98 (31560)

Congratulations!

You're now ready to try the following books in the *Recorder from the Beginning* scheme by John Pitts:

Recorder from the Beginning Book 3

Pupil's Book EJ10008
Pupil's Book + CD accompaniment EJ10057
The next book in the course, developing further musical skills and recorder techniques.

Recorder Duets from the Beginning

Pupil's Book 1 CH61213
Pupil's Book 2 CH61214
Pupil's Book 3 CH61215
Three books of easy duets for descant recorders, graded to be used alongside the course.

Descant & Treble Recorder Duets from the Beginning

Pupil's Book CH61297
Easy mixed duets for descant and treble recorders to play together.

Recorder Trios from the Beginning

Pupil's Book CH61422
For different combinations of recorders:
two descants and treble
descant and two trebles
descant, treble and tenor.

Recorder from the Beginning Blues, Rags & Boogies

Pupil's Book CH61383
A fun collection of graded pieces which will appeal to everyone!

Treble Recorder from the Beginning

Pupil's Book EJ10003
For descant players reaching the end of *Recorder from the Beginning* Book 1 or equivalent.

Teacher's Books are available to accompany all these books

Available from all good music shops,
or in case of difficulty please contact:

Music Sales Limited
(Education Department)
Newmarket Road, Bury St Edmunds
Suffolk IP33 3YB

10/01 (41780)